The Little Book of
NORTH
AMERICAN
BIRDS

**BUSHEL
& PECK
BOOKS**

The Little Book of
NORTH AMERICAN BIRDS

CHRISTIN FARLEY

CONTENTS

While experts at finding nectar, their food of choice, hummingbirds have another amazing trait: memory! They can remember every flower they have ever visited, not to mention their migration routes, which can extend for hundreds or thousands of miles and will be undertaken as a solo journey. Perhaps not surprising, hummingbirds have big brains, which are proportionally among the largest of any birds on earth.

Rufous
Hummingbird

1. HUMMINGBIRD

"Iridescent" and "tireless" describe these smallest of the world's birds. Known for their slight stature, hummingbirds are on the constant hunt for food, and while zipping about, they bring stunning beauty to the world around them. Whether migrating long distances or flitting around your backyard bird feeder, these birds can catch your eye with their darting movements and array of colors. They are part of the *Trochilidae* family of avian birds but prefer to live solitary lives in the Western hemisphere.

CLASSIFICATION

KINGDOM: *Animalia*

PHYLUM: *Chordata*

CLASS: *Aves*

ORDER: *Apodiformes*

FAMILY: *Trochilidae (Hummingbirds)*

BY THE NUMBERS

1,000– 2,000	*Number of flowers visited each day.*
300+	*Known number of species of hummingbirds.*
1,200 MILES	*Distance a Ruby-throated hummingbird can fly without stopping during migration.*

FANCY FLIERS
Amazingly agile, hummingbirds are dynamic fliers. They can fly backwards, upside down, or hover in the air like a helicopter, all while flapping their wings at speeds of up to eighty beats per second.

Black-Chinned Hummingbird

FAMILY FRIENDLY

During the winter months, robins stick together, but it's not just a small family gathering. Robins commonly gather in the hundreds and can be found under bridges, in barns, or in communal trees.

American
Robin

3

1

2

2. ROBIN

Known for their beautiful songs and bright orange bellies, robins are easy to pick out in nature. One of their distinguishing characteristics is their running and stopping behavior while searching for food. They are generally found worldwide and are common visitors in North American backyards. They are so popular in North America that they have been adopted as the state bird for Connecticut, Michigan, and Wisconsin in the U.S. Robins bring new hope and cheer. Their appearance in late winter is a sign that spring is just around the corner!

BY THE NUMBERS

2,900 — A robin's feather count.

32 MILES PER HOUR — The top speed a robin can fly.

6 YEARS — Lifespan of a robin.

TREAT TIME!
Just like humans, robins have a love of sweets. Though they do eat small insects and seeds, robins enjoy berries, apples slices, raisins, and even sweet cakes. If you feel like sharing, just make sure to cut fruits into small pieces for the birds to eat.

*Northern
Cardinal
(Male)*

WHAT'S IN A NAME?

Northern cardinals are known for their bright red feathers. But where did their name come from? This bird was named after Roman Catholic Cardinals (religious leaders), as their red robes resembled the red feathers on the cardinal bird.

*Northern
Cardinal
(Female)*

3. CARDINAL

Cardinals are part of the *Cardinalidae* family and are known for their bright red plumage with black around their stout beaks. They are mostly found in North and South America and do not migrate. Cardinals will usually live about a mile from where they hatched. Lifelong mates, male and female cardinals will even sing together in cheery duets! Cardinals were chosen as the mascot for professional sports teams and the state bird for seven US states.

CLASSIFICATION

KINGDOM: *Animalia*

PHYLUM: *Chordata*

CLASS: *Aves*

ORDER: *Passeriformes*

FAMILY: *Cardinalidae*

GENUS: *Cardinalis* (Cardinals)

BY THE NUMBERS

EYE SPY

Not all cardinals are red. If you are lucky enough, you might spot a yellow cardinal in the eastern United States. or eastern Canada. With only ten to twelve yellow cardinals around each year, these birds are incredibly rare.

Yellow Cardinal

24	*Number of different songs that cardinals sing.*
42 GRAMS	*Average weight of a cardinal, which is a little less than a chicken egg.*
19	*Number of cardinal subspecies.*

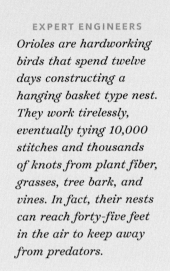

EXPERT ENGINEERS

Orioles are hardworking birds that spend twelve days constructing a hanging basket type nest. They work tirelessly, eventually tying 10,000 stitches and thousands of knots from plant fiber, grasses, tree bark, and vines. In fact, their nests can reach forty-five feet in the air to keep away from predators.

Baltimore Oriole (Male)

Baltimore Oriole (Female)

4. ORIOLE

When you see an oriole for the first time, you'll quickly realize why its name comes from the Latin word *aureolus*, meaning "golden." These flashy songbirds draw attention throughout North America and the upper region of South America. Something unusual about the oriole is that the male oriole has a unique, one-of-a-kind song that its mate can pick out and identify. Orioles also play an important role in pollinating many tree species while in their tropical winter habitat; pollen gets transferred from tree to tree by orioles are eating nectar.

CLASSIFICATION

KINGDOM: *Animalia*

PHYLUM: *Chordata*

CLASS: *Aves*

ORDER: *Passeriformes*

FAMILY: *Icteridae*

GENUS: *Icterus*
(New World orioles)

FINE DINING

Another curious fact about orioles is their peculiar taste for hairy caterpillars, like the tent caterpillar (left). While most birds find these caterpillars hard to swallow because of the hair, the oriole solves the problem by banging the caterpillar against a tree to remove the hair. Perfect problem solving!

BY THE NUMBERS

45	*Number of grasshoppers a bullock oriole can eat in one day.*
12 DAYS	*Amount of time it takes an oriole to build its nest.*
11 YEARS	*Maximum lifespan of an oriole.*

13

TRICKY TONGUE

When you think of long tongues, you might think of animals like chameleons or frogs. However, the tongue length of a woodpecker is also impressive; it's twice as long as its beak! This is a useful tool when hunting hard-to-reach bugs in the crevices of a pecked-out tree. When not in use, woodpecker tongues curl around the back of the head between the skin and skull.

Ivory-Billed
Woodpecker

Downy
Woodpecker

5. WOODPECKER

It's no surprise that woodpeckers make their home in wooded habitats. They can be found nearly worldwide and even in the rainforest. Woodpeckers are a common favorite among bird enthusiasts, and they're both resourceful and intelligent. By drumming their beaks, they make reverberating sounds that can communicate with other woodpeckers. The drumming is also a way they build their home, which is often a cozy hole carved into a tree. They are perfectionists when it comes to that hole and will continue to peck at it until the entrance is a perfect circle. Each year, woodpeckers find a new home to make, leaving their previous hole for another bird species to use.

CLASSIFICATION

KINGDOM: *Animalia*

PHYLUM: *Chordata*

CLASS: *Aves*

ORDER: *Piciformes*

INFRAORDER: *Picides*

FAMILY: *Picidae*
(*Woodpeckers, piculets, wrynecks, and sapsuckers*)

BY THE NUMBERS

1,200	*Number of times a woodpecker can peck a day.*
18	*Number of woodpecker species threatened with extinction.*
2	*Number of toes facing forward and backward, which makes it easier to hold onto a tree.*

HARD-HEADED

If you banged your head against a tree for hours a day, you would get a concussion! This is not the case with woodpeckers. They pack a force of 1,000 g in each hit to the tree, and it doesn't even cause a headache. In comparison, less than 100 g of force can cause a brain injury to a football player.

Most bird species have a diet that consists of things like berries, insects, or even nuts and fruit. Goldfinches, however, have a specific diet of almost entirely seeds! Their favorites are thistle and sunflower seeds.

American
Goldfinch

6. GOLDFINCH

Goldfinches are highly social birds that gather by the thousands to migrate together in the autumn. They gained great popularity during the 1700s, and their name was even used as slang to describe someone with great wealth. Goldfinches also appear in medieval paintings as a symbol of fertility and resurrection. Usually, goldfinches will try to rear two to three brood every year, even though they also might migrate in the winter. During winter, male goldfinch feathers turn a dull gray and brown, allowing them to hide from predators. Once spring comes, they molt into their brilliant yellow plumage!

BY THE NUMBERS

5	*Usual number of greenish-blue eggs goldfinches lay at a time.*
12 DAYS	*How long it takes for goldfinch eggs to hatch.*
3	*Number of existing goldfinch species (American, Lesser, and Lawrence goldfinches).*

HANGING AROUND

Impressively, a goldfinch can feed upside down! You might see them hanging from the top of a sunflower and plucking out the seeds below.

Chickadees are savvy savers. They know that food can be a scarce resource, so chickadees will store food in different hiding spots, like crevices in bark. Somehow, they're able to remember thousands of hiding places over time.

Chestnut-
Backed
Chickadee

7. **CHICKADEE**

Commonly found in wooded areas across North America, the chickadee gets its name from the distinctive alarm call they sound: "chick-a-dee-dee-dee!" The number of "dees" in the call depends upon the type of predator. These small, non-migratory birds are big fans of man-made feeders. While they consume nature's abundance of insects and seeds, they still get about 20% of their food from feeders. That's one reason you might see some ravenous eaters enjoying your backyard feeder, especially if you have sunflower seeds!

KINGDOM: *Animalia*

PHYLUM: *Chordata*

CLASS: *Aves*

ORDER: *Passeriformes*

FAMILY: *Paridae*

GENUS: *Poecile*
(*Chickadees and tits*)

BY THE NUMBERS

27	*Number of times their wings beat per second.*
2 STATES	*Number of states with chickadees as their state bird (Massachusetts and Maine).*
12 YEARS	*Record lifespan of a chickadee.*

Northern Chickadee

EAGER EATERS
Cold winter nights bring a challenge for chickadee survival. They can lose 10% of their body weight each night trying to stay warm. As a result, these birds need twenty times the amount of food in the winter than in the summer.

Bluebirds are territorial and protective. The females will generally defend the nest site while the males will protect the territory edges. These monogamous birds make a great team!

Mountain
Bluebird
(Male)

Mountain
Bluebird
(Female)

8. BLUEBIRD

Also known as thrushes, bluebirds are popular songbirds who prefer living in open areas where they can fly freely. They raise their young in nesting cavities, like the ones abandoned by woodpeckers. The mortality rate of the bluebird is high, with only about 30% surviving their first year of life. This is partly due to high competition in the wild for natural cavities in which to build protected nests. However, with the help of man-made, artificial nesting boxes, bluebirds are making a comeback.

CLASSIFICATION

KINGDOM: *Animalia*

PHYLUM: *Chordata*

CLASS: *Aves*

ORDER: *Passeriformes*

FAMILY: *Turdidae*

GENUS: *Sialia (Bluebirds)*

Eastern Bluebird

OPTICAL ILLUSION

Bluebirds are not really blue! There is no blue pigment in their feathers. Instead, the blue we see comes from the way light waves interact with protein molecules (keratin) in the feathers.

BY THE NUMBERS

20 DAYS	*Time it takes a bluebird to first fly after hatching.*
50 YARDS	*Distance a bluebird can spot insects in tall grass.*
12%	*Amount of their body weight bluebirds consume a day.*

21

DANGEROUS DEGREES

The principal threat to the wren is not a predator or carnivorous animal, but cold weather. Because they don't migrate to warmer climates, wrens are especially susceptible to sub-zero temperatures and snow. During winter, you might see them huddling together to stay warm.

Marsh Wren

9. WREN

If you've ever spotted a tiny, round, brown bird with long legs and short wings, you've probably seen a wren. These high energy birds fly fast and low to the ground. The wren is found from Alaska and Canada down to Argentina, with the highest variety living in the neotropics. Though the wren might be one of the smallest birds, it makes up for size with its volume. Compared with a crowing rooster, the Pacific wren produces ten times the decibel-to-body-size ratio of sound. Now that's a set of lungs!

BY THE NUMBERS

10 CENTIMETERS	*Average length of a wren.*
88	*Number of wren species.*
60	*Number of wrens found in one nesting box during an extremely cold winter.*

House
Wren

23

Sparrows are fast flyers. How fast? Fast enough to beat any Olympian in a race! Sparrows can fly up to thirty-one miles per hour, which is quicker than any human has ever run on record.

Field
Sparrow

10. SPARROW

Sparrows are diverse, social birds and can be found worldwide. In North America alone there are thirty-five different sparrow species. By nature, sparrows are carnivorous birds. But due to human interaction, sparrow diets have changed over time to include berries and seeds as well. Sparrows gather in large groups and are not usually territorial unless they are protecting their nests. These nests are found in tree hollows or under bridges and roofs. Though sparrows have a more modest appearance, especially compared with other birds, their large feet might catch your eye as they use them to rummage for seeds.

MAKING A SPLASH

Bird baths are common in backyards, but have you ever seen a bird actually swim? It turns out that sparrows can, especially if they must escape predators—even underwater! Ironically, though, they bathe themselves in . . . dirt.

CLASSIFICATION

KINGDOM: *Animalia*

PHYLUM: *Chordata*

CLASS: *Aves*

ORDER: *Passeriformes*

SUPERFAMILY: *Emberizoidea*

FAMILY: *Passerellidae*
(New World sparrows)

BY THE NUMBERS

5 YEARS	*Average lifespan of a sparrow in the wild.*
6 INCHES	*Typical length of a sparrow.*
15 DAYS	*Amount of time young sparrows stay in the nest before leaving.*

Olive
Warbler

STICKY SITUATIONS
While most birds hunt for insects and spiders, the warbler has to be particularly careful. They have been known to get caught in the webs of orb spiders and meet their demise.

11. WARBLER

A warbler can be any of the small songbirds belonging to the *Parulidae* family. Warblers come in many colors. Some are dressed in subtle colors like browns or grays, while others have brightly colored plumage. Warblers are mostly found in marshes, gardens, and woodlands, where they hunt for moths, mosquitos, and beetles. These jittery birds are always on the move and complete long migrations from the West Indies and South America up to Canada and back. Resourceful as well, warblers construct their nests from deer hair, bark, and grass.

CLASSIFICATION

KINGDOM: *Animalia*

PHYLUM: *Chordata*

CLASS: *Aves*

ORDER: *Passeriformes*

SUPERFAMILY: *Emberizoidea*

FAMILY: *Parulidae*
(New World warblers)

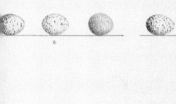

JELLYBEANS?
Warblers lay between one to seven eggs in each brood. Their eggs look like greenish-white, candy-coated jellybeans with brown speckles.

BY THE NUMBERS

0.5 OUNCES	*Weight that a warbler can reach, which is the same weight as a pencil.*
11 YEARS	*Age of the oldest surviving warbler on record.*
7.2 INCHES	*Height of the tallest warbler.*

27

Blue Jay

COPYCATS

Red-shouldered hawks are a blue jay's chief predators. To protect themselves and other birds from being a hawk's next meal, the blue jay will imitate the sound of the hawk once it is spotted as a sort of alarm system.

12. BLUE JAY

O ne of the most recognizable songbirds is the blue jay. Known for its blue plumage, black accents, and white underbelly, male and females are almost indistinguishable from each other. They may not be the fastest flyers, but blue jays are highly intelligent. Resourceful and opportunistic, these birds will patiently wait while you finish your lunch and then swoop down to enjoy your leftovers. If you are a farmer, they don't mind waiting for you to finish spreading seeds before they come to help themselves. Members of the *Corvidae* family, blue jays are considered by scientists to be some of the smartest animals on earth.

CLASSIFICATION

KINGDOM: *Animalia*

PHYLUM: *Chordata*

CLASS: *Aves*

ORDER: *Passeriformes*

FAMILY: *Corvidae*

GENUS: *Cyanocitta (Jays)*

BY THE NUMBERS

26 YEARS	*Oldest blue jay age ever recorded.*
3 OUNCES	*Weight of a blue jay, which is the same as a deck of playing cards.*
15 INCHES	*A blue jay's wingspan.*

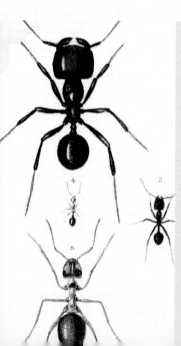

ACIDIC ANTS

Blue jays love to feed on ants, but before they begin their meal, they rub the ants on their feathers. The process is known as "anting," and it drains the ants of their formic acid, making them more edible. Smart birds!

Martins commonly feed on flying insects like dragonflies and beetles, but they also consume insects more dangerous to humans like wasps and winged ants.

Purple
Martin

13. PURPLE MARTIN

You might not have heard of martins before, but "martin" is a name for a variety of swallows in the *Hirundinidae* family. The purple martin is the largest and most common of these in North America. In winter, these birds migrate to the Amazon Basin, but in other parts of the year, they can be found closer to home in open areas near wetlands, wet meadows, and swamps. Amazingly, martins usually make it back to the exact same nesting site each year. If you are lucky enough to find one in your backyard during warmer months, it's easy to identify: it's the only swallow with a dark belly in all of North America.

STOMACHACHE

From a young age, baby martins have tough stomachs. This is because their parents feed them shards of glass and metal. This strengthens the nestlings' gizzards so they can tear apart sharp exoskeletons of hard-bodied insects later. Tough love!

CLASSIFICATION

KINGDOM: *Animalia*

PHYLUM: *Chordata*

CLASS: *Aves*

ORDER: *Passeriformes*

FAMILY: *Hirundinidae*

GENUS: *Progne*

SPECIES: *P. subis (Purple martin)*

BY THE NUMBERS

1	*Rank in size among all swallows (i.e. it's the biggest!).*
45 MILES PER HOUR	*Flying speed of a purple martin.*
13 YEARS	*Age of the oldest known purple martin.*

31

Mourning
Dove

SAVVY STORAGE

No one likes to miss out on a good meal. Mourning doves will store extra seeds in a special place in their esophagus called a "crop." Once, a mourning dove was found with 12,700 bluegrass seeds crammed in its crop!

14. MOURNING DOVE

The mourning dove, also known as the turtle dove, gets its name from the mournful cooing sound it makes, but there is nothing sad about these birds! Male and female mourning doves can be seen cuddling together, as they are often lifelong mates. Together, they can raise up to six broods a year. Mourning doves hunt diligently for seeds, which make up 99% of their diet. You can find these birds almost anywhere, from the Mojave Desert to southern Canada to northern Mexico. They can even be seen flying in a tight formation during breeding season.

BY THE NUMBERS

2	*Number of eggs per brood.*
20%	*Percentage of their body weight they must eat each day.*
70 MILLION	*Number lost each year to game hunting.*

THIRST QUENCHER
All birds need water to survive, so how can they thrive in the desert? Incredibly, mourning doves can drink brackish spring water— water that has more salt than fresh water but less salt than ocean water— without becoming dehydrated like humans.

Did you know that crows hold funerals? When a crow discovers another crow's dead body, it calls out for other crows to congregate. Together, they make a lot of noise like they are discussing what could have caused its demise. These events are called "wakes."

American
Crow

15. CROW

Crows are some of the most intelligent animals on earth, and when it comes to smarts, they are even considered on par with chimpanzees. Their brain-to-body size ratio is greater than that of any bird—even greater than humans! They are part of the *Corovidea* family and so are known as corvids. This family of birds also includes ravens, which are easy to confuse with crows (hint: ravens are larger). Crows have an unusual gift that's unique among all birds: scientific studies have shown that crows not only remember human faces, but that they can retain those memories for years if those faces are seen at least twice in a year. Smarty pants!

BY THE NUMBERS

250	*Number of different calls a crow can make. It's a regular ole jukebox!*
18 INCHES	*Average height of a crow.*
4 POUNDS	*Typical weight of a crow.*

WHAT'S IN A NAME?

A group of crows is called a "murder," though it's unclear why it earned that label.

Male blackbirds have an amusing way of getting a date. To attract a female, the male crow runs around wildly with head-bowing movements while singing a low, strangled song.

Red-Winged
Blackbird
(Male)

16. BLACKBIRD

Blackbirds are songbirds that originated in Eurasia and belong to the thrush family. With thirteen subspecies of blackbird, they can be found worldwide (except for Antarctica). Unlike many birds, blackbirds build their nests on the ground. They do roost in trees, too; in fact, up to one million blackbirds have been found to roost in one area! For their diet, blackbirds eat mostly insects, berries, seeds, and worms. Occasionally, they will snack on lizards and small amphibians. Though known to pester farmers' crops, blackbirds also help by eating pesky insects and weed seeds.

BY THE NUMBERS

50 MILLION	*Estimated number of blackbird pairs in Europe.*
3 YEARS	*Typical lifespan of a blackbird.*
3	*Number of broods a crow can have per year.*

OPPOSITES ATTRACT

Similar to many types of birds, male and female blackbirds have completely different coloring. Females have a brown body with streaks on their breasts. Males have black bodies, bright yellow beaks, and golden rings around the eyes.

Red-Winged Blackbird (Female)

Starling

FOLLOW THE LEADER
Starlings sometimes swarm in huge groups in something called a murmuration. Acting almost like a school of fish, you'll see large masses of starlings flying in tight, synchronous motions. It's an amazing spectacle in the sky!

17. STARLING

Starlings are social songbirds with distinctive coloring: iridescent feathers that appear metallic! Add in those characteristic white spots, and starlings are pretty easy to identify. Their diet is made up primarily of insects and seeds, but they are not opposed to bird feeders. Due to their diet, starlings have been known to be helpful in dispersing seeds in Africa and Asia, perhaps through their droppings. Migration can vary for starlings depending on their location. Those located in northern areas will usually migrate in the fall, while those in the south will usually stay settled in their same location.

KINGDOM: *Animalia*

PHYLUM: *Chordata*

CLASS: *Aves*

ORDER: *Passeriformes*

SUBORDER: *Passeri*

FAMILY: *Sturnidae (Starlings)*

STAR POWER
Starlings can sing just fine, but they have another vocal talent: they can mimic the sounds of other birds and humans! They've even been known to copy mechanical sounds like a car alarm.

BY THE NUMBERS

21
CENTIMETERS
Average length of a starling.

85
GRAMS
Approximate weight of a starling, which is like eighty-five small paper clips.

12
DAYS
Time it takes for a starling to hatch.

39

Canada
Goose

Canada geese don't start to court until they are two to three years old. They search out a goose their same size and then mate for life, which can range from twenty to twenty-five years!

18. CANADA GOOSE

The Canada goose is especially notable for its flying V-formation while migrating (and the honking that goes with it!). Geese take turns leading the formation, where the air resistance is strongest, and resting towards the back, where they can drift on the lift made by those ahead. A female is known as a goose and a male is called a gander. They are mostly found in North America and live near ponds, parks, and lakes. As areas become more populated, Canada geese have started migrating less and have taken a liking to large, manicured lawns and man-made ponds. Most natural predators don't live in these urban areas, so as far as the geese are concerned, it's heaven.

BACK OFF, BUSTER!

You don't want to mess with the young of a goose. If a parent senses a threat to the goslings or their nest, the goose may attack. Their honking, slapping of wings, and hissing serves as a warning, but they'll bite if they have to!

BY THE NUMBERS

40 FEET	*Depth of water a goose can dive into.*
1,500 MILES	*Distance a group of Canada geese can travel in one day.*
20 POUNDS	*Weight of a typical Canada goose.*

41

DIRTY BUSINESS

Did you know that turkey vultures
pee on their legs . . . on purpose?
It's true, and there's a reason!
This is called urohidrosis, and it
helps cool the vulture off in the hot
weather. Plus, scientists believe that
the urine might kill any bacteria
on the vulture's legs as well. Smart
thinking, but you probably shouldn't
try it at home.

Turkey
Vulture

19. TURKEY VULTURE

Y ou've probably seen turkey vultures flying above dead animals, called carrion, while sporting their red featherless heads, yellow feet, and large black-brown bodies. While they sometimes get a bad rap for consuming carrion, vultures actually play an essential role in maintaining healthy ecosystems. They are the only scavenger bird that can't kill their own prey, but they can smell carrion just twelve to twenty-four hours after death. Each time they eat, they act as nature's garbage disposal and prevent the spread of disease to humans and animals by ridding the ground of dangerous animal carcasses. We owe them our thanks!

CLASSIFICATION

KINGDOM: *Animalia*

PHYLUM: *Chordata*

CLASS: *Aves*

ORDER: *Accipitriformes*

FAMILY: *Cathartidae*

GENUS: *Cathartes*

SPECIES: *C. aura (Turkey vulture)*

BY THE NUMBERS

4 POUNDS	*Typical weight of a turkey vulture.*
6 FEET	*Wingspan of a turkey vulture.*
20 YEARS	*Typical lifespan of a turkey vulture in the wild.*

TRICKY TACTIC

No vulture wants to get picked on by a predator. As a form of self-defense, turkey vultures will vomit on their assailants, sometimes spewing a distance of ten feet in order to protect themselves. Gross! But then, who are we to say?

43

FURRY FINDINGS

Does your dog shed? If he sheds outside, then he is helping titmice build their nests! Male and female titmice work together to build their nests, and they love to line them with soft materials like dog hair.

Tufted Titmouse

20. **TITMOUSE**

A titmouse is a small songbird with a mostly gray body, black forehead, and gray, mo -like crest on its head. Native to North America, these birds prefer to live in forests and woodlands, or if their habitats are disrupted, can settle for parks and gardens. Titmice will search the ground for nuts, berries, and seeds, but spend the majority of their time in trees to stay safe from predators. Deserted woodpecker homes make suitable nesting sites for titmice, since they cannot make tree cavities themselves. Providing pleasant melodies from their perches, these non-migratory birds are a delight to spot in nature!

BY THE NUMBERS

2 YEARS	*Typical lifespan of a titmouse.*
1 INCHES	*Length of a titmouse egg.*
1.5%	*Percentage of species population growth each year, which is a healthy amount!*

FELINE FACTOR

Like other birds, titmice face several predators, including snakes, raccoons, and squirrels. However, their number one nemesis is the domestic cat. Cats kill between one and four billion songbirds every year!

LIGHTWEIGHTS

When you see herons up close, you may be surprised at how tall they are. They can grow as tall as a third-grade student, but amazingly, they only weigh the same as a newborn baby!

Great Blue
Heron

21. HERON

You can usually recognize a heron from its S-shaped neck, sharp bill, and long legs. Depending on the species, these carnivores can have gray, white, brown, or black plumage. Herons mainly feed on fish, but they also eat frogs, small mammals, and reptiles from salt or freshwater sources. They're cunning hunters and have been known to attract fish by tossing seeds or fruit into the water. When it's mealtime, their bill acts like a dagger to stab their prey before they swallow it whole. Herons must be careful when eating because they can choke on prey that is too big to fit down their throats.

BY THE NUMBERS

64	*Number of different heron species.*
11 POUNDS	*Pounds of fish that a heron can eat per day.*
60 INCHES	*Height of the largest heron species, the Goliath Heron.*

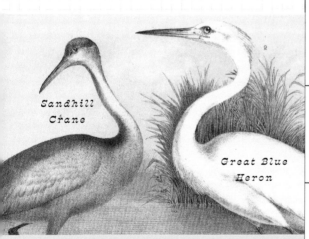

Sandhill Crane

Great Blue Heron

LOOKALIKES

It's easy for a heron to get mistaken for a crane. After all, they both have long bills, legs, and necks. The key difference is their neck shape when in flight. Herons curve their necks into an S-shape, while a crane's neck stays straight.

Baby birds are ready to leave the nest in twelve days after birth. Why so soon? It's difficult for a mother and father bird to keep the babies fed, so the chicks are motivated to learn to fly so they can feed themselves.

Northern Mockingbird

22. MOCKINGBIRD

Mockingbirds are skilled singers that are known for their ability to copy the sounds and calls of other animals. In fact, *Mimus polyglottos*, meaning "many tongued mimic," is the Latin name for mockingbirds. If you live in areas of North America where land is open and trees are sparse, there is a good chance you could see a mockingbird in your backyard. Their diet consists of insects, fruit, and seeds, though they are especially fond of seeds. Just keep your distance from their nests; mockingbirds are territorial and may come looking for a fight if they see you as a threat.

CLASSIFICATION

KINGDOM: *Animalia*

PHYLUM: *Chordata*

CLASS: *Aves*

ORDER: *Passeriformes*

FAMILY: *Mimidae (Mockingbirds, thrashers, tremblers, and catbirds)*

BY THE NUMBERS

9 INCHES	*Height of a mockingbird, which is similar to the length of a banana.*
2 OUNCES	*Typical weight of a mockingbird, which is about the same as a tennis ball.*
200	*Number of songs that mockingbirds can learn!*

49

Red-
Shouldered
Hawk

STUNNING SPECTACLE

*Many bird species
have an entertaining
courting dance, but
hawks really put on a
show. Their dance is a
ten-minute acrobatic
spectacle that includes
circular flight patterns
and ends with a
freefall back down to
the ground.*

23. HAWK

Hawks are birds of prey that typically hunt during the day (which is called being diurnal, the opposite of nocturnal). Their sharp talons and strong beaks enable them to be efficient hunters. Hawks are not picky eaters and will hunt whatever is available: small mammals, insects, reptiles, and even crustaceans. They can be found throughout the globe (except for Antarctica). Hawks generally prefer a solitary life, though in some migrating hawk species, they can be found to congregate in larger flocks, called "kettles," for warmth.

Swainson's Hawk

KNOW YOUR ENEMIES

It's a fact that hawks are great hunters. But who hunts the hunter? Adult hawks don't have many natural predators, but young hawks are susceptible to eagles, crows, owls, porcupines, snakes, and raccoons.

CLASSIFICATION

KINGDOM: *Animalia*

PHYLUM: *Chordata*

CLASS: *Aves*

ORDER: *Accipitriformes*

FAMILY: *Accipitridae*
(Hawks, eagles, kites, goshawks, and sparrowhawks)

BY THE NUMBERS

8	*Hawk eyesight is eight times better than human eyesight!*
3 FEET	*Average width of a hawk nest.*
150 MILES PER HOUR	*Speed of a diving hawk. Now that's lightning!*

Grouse are naturally equipped to survive in cold weather. Their thick plumage helps retain body heat, and it's everywhere. You can find feathers on their toes, legs, and even nostrils! The feathered toes even act like snowshoes to stay on top of the snow.

Dusky
Grouse

24. GROUSE

Grouse are experts at camouflage. Their flecked feathers can be red, brown, or gray and are covered with many bars and spots—perfect for blending in among grasses and plants. Grouse belong to the pheasant family and can vary in size. The smallest bird weighs less than one pound, while the largest can weigh fourteen pounds! Sadly, millions of grouse die each year from habitat destruction and hunting. Thankfully, however, grouse reproduce so quickly that they can replenish their numbers without too much loss. You can find these birds in cold climates and as far north as the Arctic Circle.

BY THE NUMBERS

10 INCHES	*How far down in the snow a grouse will hide to insulate in the winter.*
6 INCHES	*Nest width in inches.*
14	*Maximum number of eggs a female grouse can lay in a clutch.*

YOUNG AND RESTLESS

Young grouse are known for making quite a stir. In the fall, they are crazy fliers. People have reported them flying into office windows, homes, and even head-on into cars!

*If you were an English gentleman in the 1800s and were
rich or from royal blood, you probably participated
in pheasant hunts. This was a popular hobby for the
aristocracy. Nowadays, pheasants are protected in Britain
and can only be hunted in specific seasons.*

Common
Pheasant
(Male)

25. PHEASANT

Pheasants are beautiful birds and often used as a symbol of good luck. Widely found in North America, Europe, and Asia, pheasants originated in China. Their natural predators are coyotes, foxes, and dogs. Their most common killers, however, are humans, who hunt them for their meat and feathers. Pheasants are unique from other birds in many ways. They spend most of their lives on the ground and tend to run more than fly. Male pheasants, called cocks, can be the mate of up to seven females in one mating season. Their flashy colors and large size distinguish them from females.

Common Pheasant (Female)

MOTHERLY INSTINCTS

Pheasants are known to have large numbers of chicks. The female rears the chicks on her own and will even adopt abandoned or lost chicks from another brood.

CLASSIFICATION

KINGDOM: *Animalia*

PHYLUM: *Chordata*

CLASS: *Aves*

ORDER: *Galliformes*

FAMILY: *Phasianidae*

SUBFAMILY: *Phasianinae (Pheasants, grouse, and turkeys)*

BY THE NUMBERS

12	*Average number of eggs in a clutch.*
80 DAYS	*How long a chick is dependent on its mother.*
1.25 MILES	*Distance a pheasant can fly at one time. These are not marathon fliers!*

DUMPSTER DIVERS

Gulls are not picky eaters in the slightest. They will eat just about anything, which is why they are sometimes referred to as "garbage birds." Besides their normal fish and insects, gulls will also eat dead animals and other birds' eggs.

Glaucous
Gull

Short-Billed
Gull

26. GULL

Gulls, colloquially known as seagulls, are members of the *Laridae* family. With fifty species of gulls throughout the world, there's quite a bit of variety. Though these seabirds are commonly found near oceans and other coastlines, some live in different habitats far from water, like deserts! The smallest gull can weigh 4.2 ounces, while the largest can weigh almost 4 pounds. Incredibly, gulls can drink both fresh *and* saltwater. They have special glands near their eyes that allow them to flush the salt from their system through openings in their bill. Cool, right?

BY THE NUMBERS

15-20 YEARS	*Average lifespan of a seagull in the wild.*
50	*Number of species found worldwide.*
20%	*Percentage of body weight a gull must eat a day.*

BALANCING ACT
Have you ever seen a seagull standing on one leg? Though it looks peculiar, it turns out that gulls do this to stay warm. Without feathers on their legs, their skin is exposed to cold air. Having one leg up while standing keeps at least one of their legs nestled in warm feathers!

Puffins are known worldwide for their vibrant orange bills. But surprisingly, this is not a permanent feature. The bill is normally a dull gray color and only changes to the unforgettable orange once mating season rolls around in the spring.

Atlantic Puffin

27. PUFFIN

They might look like adorable ten-inch penguins, but there is much more to the puffin than meets the eye! Puffins spend most of the year in the open ocean and return to home grounds once mating season begins. There, they enjoy a rich, social environment and nest in large colonies, usually with the same mate year after year. The birds in the colony protect the nesting area together, and mates share the workload of incubating their egg for close to forty-five days. Puffins are also fast fliers and remarkable swimmers. With their webbed feet, they can dive two-hundred feet underwater for fish!

HOME SWEET HOME

No less than eight islands around the world are called "Puffin Island" because they have been, or currently are, home to large colonies of puffins. If you're looking for puffins closer to home, they can be found in Maine (United States) and Newfoundland (Canada).

Northern Gannet

NOSEDIVE

Gannets are daring divers. They can reach speeds of up to 60 miles per hour when they hit the water in a dive. Thankfully, this doesn't cause injury, as a gannet's body is well-equipped to absorb the impact. A gannet's neck muscles and spongy bone at the base of its bill keep it from harm.

28. GANNET

Gannets are striking seabirds from the *Sulidae* family. They have long necks and beaks, white plumage, and black wingtips. There are three gannet species in the world. The largest of these is the Northern gannet, which is nearly the size of an Albatross! It is also the only species to live in North America. They spend the majority of their lives at sea and have only one egg per year. When they do come to land, they nest on cliff ledges or other locations with large populations of fish. Gannets don't have many natural predators, but they do have to be aware of the occasional eagle, shark, or seal that might enjoy them for a meal.

CLASSIFICATION

KINGDOM: *Animalia*

PHYLUM: *Chordata*

CLASS: *Aves*

ORDER: *Suliformes*

FAMILY: *Sulidae*

GENUS: *Morus*
(Gannets)

BY THE NUMBERS

1,000	*Number of gannets you might see feeding at one time.*
5 YEARS	*Time it takes for a gannet to reach maturity.*
17 YEARS	*Typical lifespan of a gannet.*

TREASURE HUNTERS

It's normal for a gannet nest to be constructed from feathers, mud, seaweed, and other native resources. Gannet researchers, however, have found some surprising discoveries in nest walls: golf balls, fake teeth, plastic wrap, a gold watch, and even shotgun casings!

NICE NEIGHBORS

Razorbills, guillemots, and puffins can all be found living in fairly close proximity. Does this create competition for food? No! This neighborly situation is solved because they each feed on different sizes of fish. Razorbills hunt the medium fish, guillemots aim for the large fish, and puffins go for the small fish. How's that for harmony?

Razorbill

29. RAZORBILL

Razorbills are duck-sized birds that display impressive plumage of brilliant white on the belly and black on the back, head, and beak. They live in the Northern Atlantic Ocean but come to nest on rocky, shoreline cliffs. It is believed that they are the closest living relative to the Great Auk that went extinct in the 1800s. Razorbills tend to forgo nest building. They are content to live in a nest made by a puffin or even a rabbit burrow. Crevices work well for nesting, too—anything that will protect their young from predators. They also choose locations that are close to schools of herring, sprat, and capelin.

KINGDOM: *Animalia*

PHYLUM: *Chordata*

CLASS: *Aves*

ORDER: *Charadriiformes*

FAMILY: *Alcidae*

GENUS: *Alca*

SPECIES: *A. torda (Razorbill)*

BY THE NUMBERS

41 YEARS — *Age of the oldest known razorbill.*

330 FEET — *Depth a razorbill can dive to catch fish underwater.*

3 MILES PER HOUR — *Speed a razorbill will fly during mating season. They aren't fast fliers!*

A LEAP OF FAITH

Even before they have all their feathers, razorbill chicks will jump from their nest on the edge of cliffs into the ocean, sometimes hundreds of feet below. While this doesn't seem like a wise choice, the father follows nearby to make sure his chick will be able to provide for himself in the water.

California
Condor

TWINS?

Sometimes California condors
can be confused with turkey
vultures. How can you tell
them apart? Simple: the
condor is much larger and has
a massive ten-foot wingspan.
That's giant indeed!

Turkey
Vulture

30. CALIFORNIA CONDOR

The California condor is the largest bird in North America and one of the largest birds in the world. With humongous wingspans and a vulture-like appearance, these birds are nearly impossible to miss. Part of the vulture family, condors are carrion feeders, meaning they don't hunt but instead consume dead wildlife. California condors are critically endangered animals. In the 1980s, only twenty-two were left in the wild. Today, their numbers have risen to about 300 in the wild, but that's still dangerously low. Thankfully, a conservation project is in place to help protect this important species.

CLASSIFICATION

KINGDOM: *Animalia*

PHYLUM: *Chordata*

CLASS: *Aves*

ORDER: *Accipitriformes*

FAMILY: *Cathartidae*

GENUS: *Gymnogyps*

SPECIES: *G. californianus (California condor)*

BY THE NUMBERS

10 FEET	*Length of a condor's wingspan. Wow!*
150 MILES	*Distance a condor can fly each day in search of food.*
60 YEARS	*Average lifespan of a condor.*

CLEAN FREAKS

California condors might seem dirty, but the opposite is actually true. Condors spend hours bathing. After eating, they also clean their neck and head by rubbing them on branches, rocks, or grass.

Providing for themselves and their young can be a tall order for terns. To help supplement their diets, terns have no problem stealing fish from each other or from gulls. "Finders keepers" is their motto!

Caspian
Tern

31. TERN

Terns are medium-sized birds with attractive plumage of silvery-gray on their back, a white belly, and a black cap on their head. Their bright orange bills and feet contrast beautifully against their light bodies. Terns are known for their endurance and have one of the longest migratory travels of any bird: the Arctic tern travels 25,000 miles one way from the Arctic to Antarctica every year! Terns feed on marine life, so they must live near water. They make their nests in wooded areas or rocky beaches so they don't have to go far to scoop up fish or dive into the water to find their dinner.

BY THE NUMBERS

30+ YEARS — *Typical lifespan of a tern.*

15 INCHES — *Maximum height of a tern.*

1-4 — *Number of eggs in a tern clutch.*

A TERN NEVER FORGETS

Colonies of tern can be crowded with thousands of residents. Amazingly, they can still always find their own nesting site, even if their eggs have been buried or no remains can be seen of their actual nest.

NUMEROUS NICKNAMES

A group of birds is often called a flock, but with pelicans, you have many nicknames to choose from when referring to a group of three or more. A "scoop," "pod," "brief," "pouch," or "squadron" will all work!

Brown Pelican

32. **PELICAN**

Spotting a pelican is a sure sign that you are near water. They can be found throughout the world (for Antarctica) and always close to water. Pelicans are part of the *Pelecanidae* family. Their distinguishing feature is a pouch under their bill. The pouch acts as a fishing net that lets them scoop up fish from the water. Before swallowing his fish whole, a pelican drains the water by shaking his head back and forth. Pelicans prefer warmer climates and have been observed to have unique personalities of their own. The brown pelican, one of eight total pelican species, was once endangered but has been restored through conservation efforts.

CLASSIFICATION

KINGDOM: *Animalia*

PHYLUM: *Chordata*

CLASS: *Aves*

ORDER: *Pelecaniformes*

FAMILY: *Pelecanidae*

GENUS: *Pelecanus (Pelicans)*

BY THE NUMBERS

10,000 FEET	*Maximum height a pelican can reach in flight.*
7 FEET	*A pelican's widest wingspan.*
3 GALLONS	*Amount of water a pelican pouch can hold.*

SMART HUNTERS

Pelicans are opportunistic hunters. They are known to follow close behind fishing boats in hopes of an easy lunch. They might even eat an offensive seafull!

Bald Eagle

Eagles have amazing eyesight! They can see five times better than humans. Not only can they detect ultraviolet light, but they can also see five basic colors (as opposed to a human's basic three). This sharp sight is due in part to an unusually high density of nerves around their eyes that pass high levels of information to the brain.

33. EAGLE

Majestic and powerful, eagles are the largest bird of prey in North America. One of the most famous species is the bald eagle. They have special importance to the United States as a symbol of freedom and independence. (Interestingly, Benjamin Franklin criticized the choice and felt a turkey was more the "bird of courage," though he never formally proposed it.) You can find eagles far from predators at the tops of cliffs in nests that can be eight feet wide and thirteen feet deep. Cunning hunters, eagles are equipped with a hooked beak that makes it easy to tear through the flesh of their prey, which include reptiles, birds, mammals, and fish. They mate for life.

Golden Eagle

HONORARY OFFICER

Eagles have helped British police crack down on drone-driven burglaries. Task forces have trained the eagles to take down the drones; the eagles think they are other birds taking over their territory!

CLASSIFICATION

KINGDOM: *Animalia*

PHYLUM: *Chordata*

CLASS: *Aves*

ORDER: *Accipitriformes*

FAMILY: *Accipitridae (Eagles, hawks, kites, goshawks, and sparrowhawks)*

BY THE NUMBERS

100
MILES PER HOUR

Speed of an eagle in full dive. Watch out!

60

Number of different eagle species. The most common in North America are the bald eagle, the golden eagle, the white-tailed eage, and Steller's sea eagle.

Great
Gray Owl

THE SILENT KILLER

Owls have specialized feathers that allow them to be inches from their prey before they are heard. The edge of their wing feathers have comb-like serrations that break up turbulent air, allowing for silent flight instead "swooshing" sounds.

34. OWL

Owls are mysterious, intriguing birds that belong to the bird order *Strigiformes*. While they have strikingly large eyes, it's not actually a guarantee of good eyesight. In fact, owls are naturally farsighted (meaning they can see far away but don't see well up close). They do have excellent night vision, but their hearing is what's truly remarkable. Their flat faces help to funnel sound to their ears. Their hearing is so good that owls can even catch an animal a foot under the snow without even seeing it. These expert hunters are naturally good at camouflaging and live to be around ten years in the wild.

Great
Horned Owl

HUNGER GAMES

Surviving in the wild can be rough when it comes to food. This is especially true if you are a small owl like the barred owl. Their most dangerous predator? The great horned owl—one of their own kind.

BY THE NUMBERS

270 DEGREES
Amount an owl can rotate its neck, which is almost all the whole way around!

1,000
Number of rodents a barn owl can eat in a year.

250
Number of owl species in the world.

It's a good thing quails have such large broods, because 70-80% of the quail population is depleted each year due to predators. The large broods replenish the quail's numbers and keep up a healthy population.

California
Quail

35. QUAIL

The quail belongs to the pheasant family and is easy to identify thanks to its striking plume. The quail's plume is a cluster of dark feathers that overlap on top of the head like an exclamation point. This medium-sized bird enjoys dirt baths as a way to clean its feathers. Quails eat a delicious diet of seeds, insects, and grains. Though not loud birds, quails do make a unique sound when calling to their comrades. It famously sounds like "Chi-ca-go," and it's one of the most iconic sounds of the West.

KINGDOM: *Animalia*

PHYLUM: *Chordata*

CLASS: *Aves*

ORDER: *Galliformes*

SUPERFAMILY: *Phasianoidea*

FAMILY: *Odontophoridae (New World quails)*

BY THE NUMBERS

10-12	*Number of eggs that quails lay at a time.*
95%	*Percent of a quail's diet that is plant matter.*
3.4 OUNCES	*Weight of an adult quail, which is about like an extra-small apple.*

CAN YOU SPEAK PLUME?
Body language can give you clues about how a person is feeling; a plume does the same for a quail. You can tell a quail is alert or agitated if the plume stands straight. If the plume is angled backward, then the bird is relaxed or resting.

If you are ever curious about how a turkey is feeling, look at the color of its head and neck. The color blue means the turkey is excited. If you see red, you might want to run. This means it is ready to fight!

Wild
Turkey

36. TURKEY

The turkeys we know today are mostly domesticated turkeys that originated in North America. However, that delicious bird you eat at Thanksgiving has many differences from the turkeys that live in the wild! Wild turkeys can fly fifty-five miles per hour and soar for up to a mile. They can also run up to twelve miles per hour and will roost in trees to protect themselves from predators. These old timers have been around for ten million years, and with a stable population, we'll be able to enjoy them in the wild—or on our dinner plate—for generations to come.

BY THE NUMBERS

46 MILLION	*Number of turkeys that are killed each year for Thanksgiving.*
2	*Number of times turkeys almost went extinct!*
6,000	*Number of feathers on an adult turkey.*

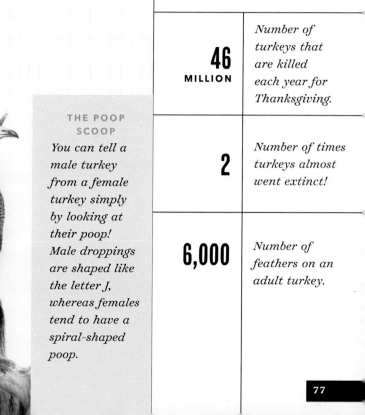

Mexican Turkey

THE POOP SCOOP

You can tell a male turkey from a female turkey simply by looking at their poop! Male droppings are shaped like the letter J, whereas females tend to have a spiral-shaped poop.

Mallard
(Female)

Though not as common as chicken eggs, duck eggs are prized for their creamy, rich taste. Farmers who raise ducks for eggs know that their hens need seventeen hours of light to produce eggs. In order to keep up production during seasons of shorter daylight, electric lights are used in their coops.

Mallard
(Male)

37. DUCK

Ducks, also known as waterfowl, are generally found near bodies of water like rivers and ponds. Well-adapted for their environment, ducks have webbed feet and waterproof feathers that make them super swimmers and keep them comfortably dry. These social omnivores tend to stick together in a large group called a paddling. Like a chicken, a female duck is called a hen, but a male is not called a rooster! Male ducks are called drakes, and they will try to attract a mate with their colorful plumage. Some of the most common ducks in North America include the mallard, American black duck, wood duck, redhead, bufflehead, and many others.

TO DAB OR TO DIVE?

One way to classify a duck is by how it eats. Ducks that feed on land or on the surface of the water are dabbling ducks. Those that submerge themselves in the water to find their next meal are known as diving ducks.

CLASSIFICATION

KINGDOM: *Animalia*

PHYLUM: *Chordata*

CLASS: *Aves*

ORDER: *Anseriformes*

SUPERFAMILY: *Anatoidea*

FAMILY: *Anatidae*
(Ducks, geese, and swans)

BY THE NUMBERS

500 YEARS	*Length of time humans have had domesticated ducks.*
20 YEARS	*Oldest recorded age of a duck.*
3	*Number of eyelids a duck has; the third is clear and acts like goggles.*

Common
Loon

*Loons need a little help
with digestion. Because
they don't have teeth,
loons will swallow small
pebbles to help smash
up their just-finished
meal. Remarkably, this
helps the food go down
more smoothly in their
digestive tract.*

38. LOON

Loons are aquatic birds. There are five different loon species, all of which live north of the equator. They have striking outfits of black speckled feathers, white undersides, and red eyes. Because of their size and shape, loons are commonly mistaken as ducks. However, loons are more closely related to albatrosses and penguins than they are to ducks. While excellent divers (they can go as deep as 230 feet!), loons are awkward on land. Their legs are set back further on their bodies than a duck's, making them appear clumsy. In fact, this is how the loon got its name! Loons make an enchanting, haunting call that is famous in the northern U.S. and Canada. The bird is even featured on the Canadian one-dollar coin, which is called—you guessed it—a loonie!

BY THE NUMBERS

2	*Number of eggs a female loon will usually lay.*
75 MILES PER HOUR	*A loon's flight speed during migration.*
5 MINUTES	*How long a loon can stay underwater.*

FEEDING FRENZY

A parent's job is never done—at least for about three months! Male and female loons share the exhausting job of feeding their chicks hourly for their chicks' first three months of life.

81

Trumpeter
Swan

39. SWAN

Swans are intelligent, majestic waterfowl and the largest bird in the *Anatidae* family. They are known for their elongated necks, white feathers, and gracefulness on the water. The majority of swans are found in the northern United States, Canada, and Alaska (their equally beautiful counterpart, the black swan, can be found in Australia and New Zealand). Swans are lifelong mates and have few natural predators. Like other large bird species, they reach maturity at a later age (around year three). All species migrate in some form and are known to fly in their famous V-formation, not unlike Canada geese.

Tundra Swan

FEAR FACTOR

In most situations, swans are harmless and non-aggressive. But if threatened, swans will act in defense of themselves and their family.

CLASSIFICATION

KINGDOM: *Animalia*

PHYLUM: *Chordata*

CLASS: *Aves*

ORDER: *Anseriformes*

FAMILY: *Anatidae*

SUBFAMILY: *Anserinae*

GENUS: *Cygnus (Swans)*

BY THE NUMBERS

25,000	*Typical number of feathers on a swan.*
20-30 POUNDS	*Average weight of a swan.*
60 MILES PER HOUR	*A swan's flying speed.*

83

THE ART OF DISTRACTION

Plovers, like other birds who use the "rodent run," are amazing actors. They can draw a predator's attention away from the nesting area by running away in a stop-and-start fashion and looking just like a vulnerable rodent.

Gray
Plover

American
Golden
Plover

40. PLOVER

With over sixty species of plovers worldwide, there is, not surprisingly, a high degree of variation in color and behavior among the birds. However, there are some general characteristics that all plovers share. Plovers are, generally speaking, on the shorter end of the height spectrum and have long legs, short beaks, and weigh only a few ounces. Their plumage can be either light or dark to best match the rocks in their habitat, which are usually beaches and tide pools. Plovers do a wonderful job eating unwanted insects, like flies, and destructive garden snails.

BY THE NUMBERS

12 INCHES	*Average height of an adult plover.*
2	*Number of clutches plovers make each year.*
5	*Largest number of speckled eggs that females can lay in one clutch.*

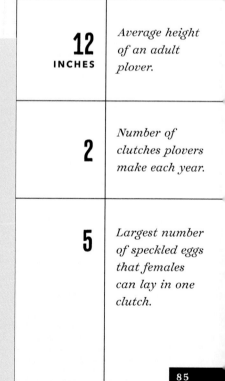

Mountain Plover

DEFEND & PRETEND

Plovers have a clever home defense against predators called "false brooding." A plover moves away from its nesting site, crouches on the ground, and pretends it's incubating a clutch of eggs. Once the predator is in close range (and away from the real nesting site), the plover hightails it away!

A PECULIAR PRACTICE

Sandpipers are known for making an odd, teetering motion while they walk, moving their rear half up and down as they shuffle along the shoreline. Scientists haven't yet figured out the reason for this motion, but that hasn't stopped the funny nicknames; sandpipers have been called "teeter-bobs," "perk birds," and "teeter-peeps."

Upland
Sandpiper

Spotted
Sandpiper

41. SANDPIPER

A sandpiper is any of the many shoreline birds that belong to the *Scolopacidae* family. The most common sandpiper in North America is the spotted sandpiper, which has beautiful, speckled plumage in warm whites and browns. The spots come and go, usually appearing strongest before breeding season. Curiously, it appears that the stronger the spotting pattern on a sandpiper, the better the bird's overall health. Sandpipers have narrow wings, short tails, and long bills and legs. They're usually found near oceans, estuaries, and tide pools, where they can forage through mud and seaweed for crustaceans, worms, and insects. Yum!

DADDY DAYCARE
Unlike many birds, sandpipers delegate most of the parental duties to the fathers! Sandpiper dads incubate the eggs (sit on the eggs to keep them warm) and take care of the babies after they hatch.

Rock Sandpiper

KINGDOM: *Animalia*

PHYLUM: *Chordata*

CLASS: *Aves*

ORDER: *Charadriiformes*

SUBORDER: *Scolopaci*

FAMILY: *Scolopacidae (Sandpipers)*

BY THE NUMBERS

4	*Normal egg count in a sandpiper clutch.*
10 YEARS	*Oldest age a sandpiper is known to have lived to.*
1,800+ MILES	*Distance a migratory sandpiper can fly nonstop.*

American
Oystercatcher

THE NAME GAME

Oystercatchers were officially named in 1731 by an English naturalist named Mark Catesby, who observed the bird's love of oysters. Previously, oystercatchers were called "sea pies." Definitely an upgrade in the name department.

42.
OYSTERCATCHER

With a name like "oystercatcher," there must be an interesting bird to go with it. There sure is! And first of all, oystercatchers don't just eat oysters. They dine on shellfish, clams, and shrimp, all of which they mostly find while wandering the shoreline or wading in shallow waters. Physical characteristics also set them apart. Most noticeable are an oystercatcher's deep orange beak, its pink legs, and the orange ring around its eyes. They really are striking birds. In order to pry open their hard-shelled meals, oystercatchers have some of the strongest bills of all shorebirds. Beauty *and* brawn—now that's something!

FREE BABYSITTING
Oystercatchers and cuckoo birds don't have much in common, except that they both "egg dump." They will purposely lay their eggs in the nest of another bird—like a gull—in hopes that the host bird will hatch and feed their young. This allows more chicks to be reared than otherwise possible.

KINGDOM: *Animalia*

PHYLUM: *Chordata*

CLASS: *Aves*

ORDER: *Charadriiformes*

SUBORDER: *Charadrii*

FAMILY: *Haematopodidae*

GENUS: *Haematopus (Oystercatchers)*

BY THE NUMBERS

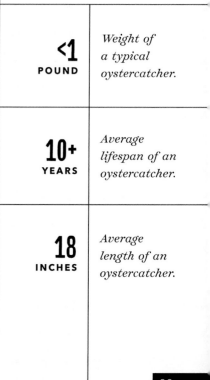

<1 POUND	*Weight of a typical oystercatcher.*
10+ YEARS	*Average lifespan of an oystercatcher.*
18 INCHES	*Average length of an oystercatcher.*

Reddish
Egret

A FAMOUS FACE

Egrets have made their mark on the world! Their faces or features are depicted on the following currency: New Zealand's 2-dollar coin, Hungary's 5-forint coin, and Brazil's 5-real banknote.

43. EGRET

Like herons, egrets belong to the *Ardeidae* family. This family of birds has long bills and curved necks, not to mention stunning all-white plumage. Egrets prefer habitats near ponds, marshes, and lakes in North and South America, Asia, and Africa. Mostly active at night, egrets prey upon almost anything living, from frogs and insects to fish and small mammals. They will stand completely still in the water, wait for their prey to approach, and then strike with their bill at lightning speed.

KINGDOM: *Animalia*

PHYLUM: *Chordata*

CLASS: *Aves*

ORDER: *Pelecaniformes*

SUBORDER: *Ardei*

FAMILY: *Ardeidae (Egrets, herons, and bitterns)*

BY THE NUMBERS

1,000	*Number of egrets that can combine into a colony.*
3 FEET	*Approximate height of a typical egret.*
4	*Average number of pale-green eggs in a clutch.*

FINE FEATHERS

Egrets were once hunted for their feathers, which were used to make fancy garments and women's hats in the early 1900s. This practice decimated the egret population, which are now protected. Thankfully, egret numbers are on the rise.

Great Egret

American
Flamingo

MILK MUSTACHE

They aren't mammals, but flamingos do create a milk-like substance from their upper digestive tracts to feed their young. Both male and females produce "crop milk," which contains red and white blood cells, fat, and protein.

44. FLAMINGO

The name flamingo originates with the Spanish and Latin word *flamenco*, meaning "fire." Their bright-colored feathers are not only glamorous, but the bold, pink color comes from a flamingo's food. Similar to ibis, flamingos feed on algae and crustaceans that have carotenoid pigments. The pigments, once ingested, create a flamingo's pink coloring. However, a flamingo's color doesn't come at birth. Several years must pass before they reach peak color and grow their distinctive curved bills. Flamingos are incredibly social birds; they congregate in a flock called a flamboyance and are always near bodies of water. Here, flamingos find mates for life and begin families with one egg per year.

CLASSIFICATION

KINGDOM: *Animalia*

PHYLUM: *Chordata*

CLASS: *Aves*

ORDER: *Phoenicopteriformes*

FAMILY: *Phoenicopteridae (Flamingos)*

DOWNWARD DIGESTION

The curve of a flamingo's bill helps filter out food from water and mud. With its head upside-down, a flamingo can sift through the mud with its feet and catch food in its bill.

BY THE NUMBERS

5 FEET	*Typical height of a flamingo.*
83	*Age of the oldest surviving flamingo.*
1958	*The first year pink plastic lawn flamingos were sold (the world has never been the same since).*

ABOUT THE AUTHOR

Christin is the author of several books for kids. She lives with her family in California, where she enjoys rollerblading, puzzles, and a good book.

BUSHEL
& PECK
BOOKS

ABOUT THE PUBLISHER

Bushel & Peck Books is a children's publishing house with a special mission. Through our Book-for-Book Promise™, we donate one book to kids in need for every book we sell. Our beautiful books are given to kids through schools, libraries, local neighborhoods, shelters, nonprofits, and also to many selfless organizations who are working hard to make a difference. So thank you for purchasing this book! Because of you, another book will find itself in the hands of a child who needs it most.

Printed in the United States
by Baker & Taylor Publisher Services